SHRIKE

a Legion Cycle play

Erin Lerch

BROADWAY PLAY PUBLISHING INC
New York
www.broadwayplaypublishing.com
info@broadwayplaypublishing.com

SHRIKE

First edition: May 2023
I S B N: 978-0-88145-986-9

Book design: Marie Donovan
Page make-up: Adobe InDesign
Typeface: Palatino

SHRIKE received its world premiere production with Fresh Ink Theatre in February 2022, after development with Fresh Ink Theatre Company, TC Squared Theatre, and Company One Theatre. The cast and creative contributors were:

SHEENA.. Emily Eldridge-Ingram
MICAH .... Jupiter Lê
HSSIK .... V Brancazio
ROACH.. Jack Chylinski
IBIS .... Alex Alexander
TSSA .... Chris Everett
AWRLL ....Alix Marie

Director.. Josh Glenn-Kayden
Dramaturg .... Alison Yueming Qu
Stage Manager .... Afrikah Selah
Assistant Stage Manager............................Winnie Chiang
Scenic design.....................................Ben Lieberson
Lighting design .... Francesca D'Angelo
Sound design..Anna Drummond
Costume design..Mikayla Reid
Makeup design .... Lynn Wilcott
Prop design ....Kelly Smith
Fight Choreographer .... Sarah Flanagan
Intimacy Director .... Ayshia Mackie-Stephenson
Video Producer (Virtual Premiere) ....Ernesto Galan

CREATIVE TEAM NOTE

SHRIKE takes place shortly into the future of the continental United States. After an alien Legion arrived and devastated human civilization via bioweapons and military might, a small band of humans continue to fight back. Grasping onto glimpses of hope over the radio, the human rebellion finds themselves fighting to survive in the face of immense grief and seemingly unbeatable odds, and to hold on to their humanity in the fight against the Legion.

To quote *Rogue One*, "Rebellions are built on hope." This rebellion has just lost Badger, who was both their indomitable leader and a beacon of hope across the resistance. Sheena finds the rebellion at this moment, as they're on the edge of falling apart in the wake of Badger's disappearance. Each member of the rebellion struggles with their own grief over the loss, leading them to clash over the question of leadership and who has the right to decide the future of the Rebellion, with Sheena caught in the middle.

When we meet her, Sheena has already lost so much, and her own grief drives much of her behavior throughout the story. She finds a mirror of her own grief in the people of the rebellion, including one person she never thought she'd connect with. In the makeshift infirmary, in a time of absolute crisis and loss, we explore the question: how do we continue to live when grief is overwhelming? How can we choose to trust when it only seems to lead to more loss?

This play is one work within Erin's Legion Cycle, which consists of multiple plays and audio dramas that all live in the same post-alien-apocalypse universe, but also each work as a standalone story. The Legion plays are intentional acts of rebellion within the American theatre. Where many institutions look for small, "producible" plays, Erin's work is ambitious, expansive, and imaginative. Where most sci-fi stories for the stage focus solely on human characters, we feature multiple alien species onstage at once. There are always numerous queer and trans actors in roles that are about more than just being queer or trans. We use the presence of nonhuman characters to investigate who has the privilege of being treated as a person, and who is seen as an outsider. We intentionally rethink brutality and violence in science fiction as our own world suffers from frequent acts of violence. We've talked about SHRIKE as the anti-Chekhov's gun—just because violence is a constant possibility in this world, does not mean it is an inevitability. There is always another choice.

In the most difficult time they've ever faced, the characters of SHRIKE still find ways to express themselves, even lightening the mood with humor. They extend trust and compassion to one another, even when it would be easier to lash out or turn away. We find that when things are feeling a little apocalyptic, a hopeful post-apocalyptic story might be just the thing to remind us that, even when things feel difficult, we can still find our way through.

—Erin Lerch (playwright), Josh Glenn-Kayden (director), Alison Yueming Qu (dramaturg), February 2022

AUTHOR'S NOTE

I think the prior note covers a lot, but I want to include a few things we've discovered while working on plays and stories in the Legion world, to help guide anyone who's ready to take on this wild sci-fi ride:

Keep in mind that this play is set in our world, in our future. The characters are as aware of science fiction stories as we are now, and they are aware that they're living through one of those stories.

Pace is incredibly important in this play. Every moment is precious. There should be no pauses where they are not noted, and if in the rehearsal room you find that it makes more sense to run through pauses that *are* noted, go right ahead. Earn the silences. Make sure they're pushing the action forward.

When designing aliens, while I've compared them loosely to Earth animals (Reptiles and canines, here), remember that they are not from Earth, and you are not limited to palettes found on Earth animals. Go nuts.

CHARACTERS & SETTING

SHEENA, *a fighter, even when she probably shouldn't be.* MICAH's *younger sister. Human. Woman, late twenties. She/her pronouns.*

MICAH, *not a fighter, even when he probably should be.* SHEENA's *older brother. Human. Trans man, late twenties/ early thirties. He/him pronouns.*

HSSIK, *pronounced "sick" on an exhale. Too fresh to be callous yet. Legion Medic. Reptilian. Probably early/mid twenties in human years. Xe/xyr pronouns.*

ROACH, *tough when they have to be, soft when they can be. Human. Nonbinary, early thirties. They/them pronouns.*

IBIS, *pronounced "eye-bis". A leader because there's no other choice. Human. Woman, sixties. She/her pronouns.*

TSSA, *pronounced "tsah", one syllable. The 'ts' is like the German letter Z sound. A former Legion Medic now working with the human resistance. Does what's right even when it's unpopular. Reptilian. Mid-late forties in human years. She/her pronouns.*

AWRLL, *Pronounced like "snarl", without the "sn". Loyal above all else. Legion Soldier. Canine. Twenties. She/her pronouns.*

There are also a number of voices that are only heard over the radio. A breakdown is included at the end of the text.

The play is split between two locations and two spaces in time.

Flashbacks occur in a dark, hidden space. Maybe a broken-down building. Maybe a cave. Maybe a collapsed overpass. Somewhere in the Upper Midwest.

The present is in one of the Rebellion's regional bases, previously run by Badger, in Lake City, Pennsylvania.

Time: The near future. Three years have passed between the past and present.

CASTING NOTE

Trans and nonbinary roles in this play must be played by trans/nonbinary actors. While I have not labeled aliens' genders as a general rule, aliens with pronouns other than she/her or he/him must be played by nonbinary actors as well. That said, actors need not necessarily use the exact same pronouns as the characters—I would encourage trans and nonbinary actors to read for any parts that they feel are appropriate. I also encourage those casting this play to think expansively about the characters who may initially read as cisgender. Unless a character is specified as cis, the role is open to anyone who feels their identity aligns with the character's.

While the characters have not been written with a specific race in mind, under no circumstances should this play have an all-white cast, nor should the only actors of color be playing nonhuman characters. As you are making casting decisions, I encourage you to consider the role of violence in this play. Consider if your casting choices are playing into harmful dynamics that already exist. Specifically, think carefully about who is pointing a gun at whom in this play.

Text note: A line break in a character's text indicates a new thought.

Scene 1

(*Lights up on what was, once upon a time, a multi-stall bathroom, and is now a makeshift infirmary. Several "beds" stand against the walls, clearly scavenged—might be fold-out couches, army cots, maybe even an inflatable mattress on a table. The room is battered but clean. Overstuffed shelves against the walls hold a wide range of medical supplies.*)

(*In one of the beds lies* SHEENA, *injured and unconscious. One arm is swathed in bandages. One eye is scarred over, maybe missing. She might have an IV, hanging from a light fixture. Nearby is* ROACH. *They are fiddling with a radio, tuning through the stations.*)

RADIO 1: —don't believe for a second she died in that crash. Badger's broken into more Legion compounds than the rest of us combined and gotten out alive. And if she did go down, she'd make sure she took as many of them as she could out with her—

RADIO 2: —still no luck making contact with anyone outside our borders. No idea if anyone's even alive out there anymore—

RADIO 3: —Badger were still alive, she'd have shown back up by now. She's not coming back. I just hope she's properly dead, not rotting in some Legion hellhole somewhere—

RADIO 4: —tracking the recent spike in Legion activity on the northwestern border with Canada. Looks like some kind of explosion; the whole mountain's burned black—

RADIO 5: —edges of the lake are still swarming with Soldiers. Hard to get close enough to see what they're doing, exactly—

RADIO 6: —three years ago today, the Legion dealt their final, devastating blow, wiping the base at Roswell off the map—

(ROACH *pauses, tunes back.*)

RADIO 5: —definitely more of them along the eastern bank, but they don't seem to be focusing in on any particular area. Seems like they haven't found anything yet, either.

ROACH: Hmm.

RADIO 7: (IBIS) Could be worse, I suppose. Is it possible they could've snuck something by you?

(SHEENA *stirs.* ROACH *turns the volume on the radio down.*)

ROACH: You're awake.

SHEENA: Wait, I want to hear that.

(ROACH *considers, then turns it back up.*)

RADIO 5: —doubt it. We've been keeping an eye on them, while the others search. If they'd found something, one of us would've noticed. A couple of folks are headed back to base to pick up more supplies.

RADIO 7: (IBIS) Just supplies?

RADIO 5: And…drop a couple of things off. Should be there in a couple of days, if the Legion cooperates.

RADIO 7: (IBIS) Understood. Keep me posted, and be careful. *(Static)*

SHEENA: You still haven't found her, huh? Badger.

ROACH: You know about her?

SHEENA: Who wouldn't?

(Pause. ROACH *turns the radio off.* SHEENA *takes in the room.)*

SHEENA: Not quite what I expected.

ROACH: What? Waking up in a bathroom?

SHEENA: Yeah. Wasn't sure I was gonna wake up at all, if I'm honest.

ROACH: Patrols found you on the side of the road north of Detroit. Was a close thing, getting you back here in time. A couple more hours and you'd've been dead.

SHEENA: Oh. Shit.

ROACH: You're lucky.

SHEENA: I guess.

ROACH: What's your name?

SHEENA: What?

ROACH: Your name?

SHEENA: It's Sheena.

ROACH: And where were you going, Sheena?

SHEENA: Here. I think. If I'm right that this is Badger's base.

ROACH: You are. Anybody else with you?

SHEENA: No. Not anymore.

ROACH: I'm sorry.

SHEENA: …Thanks.

ROACH: What happened?

SHEENA: What do you think? The Legion happened.

ROACH: And you ran here. To the Rebellion.

SHEENA: Yeah.

ROACH: Hard to travel with those injuries.

SHEENA: Which ones? The eye's pretty old by now. Some of the others, not so much.

ROACH: Arm seems pretty fresh.

SHEENA: Something you wanna know?

ROACH: Work with me, here.

(Pause)

SHEENA: Pick one. The arm, or the eye.

ROACH: What if I say both?

SHEENA: You're gonna be disappointed.

ROACH: The arm.

SHEENA: Freak accident.

ROACH: Legion accident?

SHEENA: No. Took a bad fall kind of accident.

ROACH: Uh-huh. Anybody see you?

SHEENA: If they had, I wasn't in much shape to outrun them.
So. Satisfied?

ROACH: It's a start.

SHEENA: Do I get to ask one now?

ROACH: Seems fair.

SHEENA: Where are we?

ROACH: Badger's base.

SHEENA: I got that. But where?

ROACH: Once upon a time, this was Lake City, Pennsylvania.

SHEENA: *Was*, huh?

ROACH: Now it's a ghost town. Lot of those these days.

SHEENA: No shit.

(Transition. The past. A dim, cramped space. The sound of Legion ships overhead. Streaks of dusty, dim daylight lance in through cracks in the ceiling overhead, or at a sharp angle from the doorway. SHEENA enters, half-carrying, half-dragging a badly wounded MICAH. SHEENA is uninjured.)

MICAH: Oh shit. Oh shit.

SHEENA: It's gonna be okay.

MICAH: Oh *shit*.

SHEENA: It's gonna be okay.

(SHEENA settles MICAH in the rubble and checks him over.)

SHEENA: Oh, shit.

MICAH: Told you so.

SHEENA: Okay. Uh.

MICAH: You got a plan, soldier girl?

SHEENA: Don't call me that. *(She strips off her uniform jacket and presses it against the worst of the wounds.)* Okay. Hold that there. Can you hold that?

MICAH: Yeah, I got it.

SHEENA: Good. Just. Keep holding that.

MICAH: Where are you going?

SHEENA: To find help.

MICAH: Where?

SHEENA: I'm still figuring that part out.

MICAH: Great.

SHEENA: Try not to die before I get back, okay? Asshole.

MICAH: Do my best.

(SHEENA runs out. Transition. The present. Voices outside the room. SHEENA struggles to sit up.)

ROACH: Don't, you're going to hurt yourself.

SHEENA: Ow, fuck.

ROACH: Told you.

(IBIS *enters. A moment*)

IBIS: Roach. You were supposed to come and get me when she woke up.

ROACH: I was going to.

IBIS: When, exactly?

ROACH: *(Re: the radio)* You were busy.

IBIS: Right. What did you find out?

ROACH: She came here looking for us. Alone.

IBIS: Is that all you got?

ROACH: I was working on it. Flies, honey, vinegar, et cetera.

IBIS: You're wasting time.

SHEENA: I'm right here, y'know.

IBIS: You were looking for us. Why?

SHEENA: To join up. Obviously.

(Pause)

ROACH: Obviously.

SHEENA: Why else would I come?

ROACH: That is the question, isn't it.

IBIS: How did you find us?

SHEENA: I knew you were somewhere near the Lakes.

IBIS: How?

SHEENA: The radio. I heard Badger go down, and you all searching for her. Figured I'd get close to Superior and run into you sooner or later.

ROACH: Until you got hurt.

SHEENA: Yeah.

IBIS: How did that happen?

SHEENA: Accident.

ROACH: You said that before. Think you could be a little more specific?

(Pause)

SHEENA: I cut too close to Detroit, alright? Trying to avoid the eyes in the sky. I thought I was far enough out that the blast damage wouldn't be too bad. Found out I was wrong when a bridge collapsed out from under me.

IBIS: The patrols said they found you further north.

SHEENA: Yeah. I bandaged it up, thought I was fine. Didn't realize how much blood I lost until…well. Until I woke up here.
I made a bad call. Several bad calls. That what you want to hear?

IBIS: Where were you coming from?

SHEENA: Does it matter? I'm here now.

ROACH: It matters.

SHEENA: Why? What's with the third degree? Figured you'd be happy to have the extra gun.

IBIS: We're three years into this. Why now? Why not come sooner?

(Pause)

ROACH: Sheena?

SHEENA: You have no idea how many times I've asked myself that.

IBIS: That's not an answer.

SHEENA: Oh. I get it.

IBIS: Do you?

SHEENA: You think I'm working with them. The Legion.

IBIS: For them, more like.

SHEENA: I'd *never* work for those alien fuckers.

ROACH: You've got to admit, the timing is suspicious.

SHEENA: How's that?

ROACH: Showing up just when our illustrious leader is MIA? Would be an excellent time to slip someone in under our noses.

SHEENA: And the whole almost dying thing didn't convince you?

ROACH: Wouldn't be hard to pull off with Legion tech.

SHEENA: Fine. You want me to prove I'm not a spy? Tell me what to do. I'll take whatever test you like.

(TSSA, *a Legion Medic, enters. She is reptilian, her skin scaled in muted jewel tones, and has a raised scaly crest down the back of her head and neck. She wears an incongruous pair of medical scrubs.*)

TSSA: Ibis, there you are—

(SHEENA *pulls a small pistol from under the blankets and aims it at* TSSA. ROACH *lurches between* SHEENA *and* TSSA, *blocking the shot.*)

ROACH: Easy! Easy.

SHEENA: Get out of the way.

ROACH: Put the gun down.

IBIS: I thought you disarmed her.

ROACH: The patrols said they did.

SHEENA: Move.

ROACH: Not gonna happen.

SHEENA: Why the hell are you protecting that thing?

ROACH: She's one of us.

TSSA: That "thing" has a name.

(ROACH *puts a hand on* SHEENA's *gun.*)

SHEENA: Don't. Just get out of my way.

ROACH: I'm not moving.

(ROACH *slowly push the gun down.*)

IBIS: Better.

ROACH: Thank you.

TSSA: Are we done now? Because I'd like to check on my patient.

SHEENA: What do you mean, your patient?

TSSA: I swear, humans' skulls get thicker when I'm around. *You* are my patient, and I'd like to see how your wounds are doing.

SHEENA: Over my dead body.

TSSA: It very nearly was.

SHEENA: Who the hell even are you?

TSSA: I'm the one who saved your life.

(*Transition. The past.* MICAH *lies in the rubble, his breathing shallow. The sounds of battle have receded, but the distant drone of Legion ships is almost constant.* SHEENA *enters, hauling with her a blindfolded Medic,* HSSIK, *her gun pressed to the Medic's side. A bit of fresh bruising is visible on the side of xyr head.*)

HSSIK: I'm just saying, my offer still stands. You can still let me go, we can pretend all of this never happened, and I'll make sure you aren't killed in the purge.

SHEENA: I didn't drag you all the way out here just to kill you.

MICAH: Sheena, what…?

SHEENA: I told you I was going to get help. I got help.

(SHEENA *pulls the blindfold off* HSSIK's *eyes. Xe sees* MICAH *in the rubble.*)

HSSIK: Oh.

SHEENA: Fix him.

HSSIK: What happened?

SHEENA: You did. Fix him.

HSSIK: You'd trust a Legion Medic?

SHEENA: Hell, no. But I trust my gun. And you want to live, right?

HSSIK: Yes.

SHEENA: If he dies, you die. Get to it.

(*Transition. The present*)

SHEENA: *You* saved me.

TSSA: Yes.

SHEENA: Really.

TSSA: Really.

ROACH: Really.

TSSA: Are we done? Can I check your arm now?

SHEENA: Don't touch me.

IBIS: Enough.

SHEENA: After all that about making sure I'm not a spy, you're working with the Legion?

ROACH: No. Not the Legion. Tssa's different.

TSSA: I defected.

SHEENA: Sure you did.

IBIS: Enough. Tssa's already proven her worth.

SHEENA: You know what they are, right? What they've done? They call themselves Medics, but that isn't all they do.

TSSA: To fix a body, you have to know how to take it apart.

ROACH: Not helping.

TSSA: Sorry.

IBIS: Consider this your first test. Can you follow orders, even if you don't like them?

SHEENA: I came here to follow Badger, not you.

IBIS: Badger's not here.

SHEENA: I don't even know who you are.

IBIS: Badger is—or was—my daughter.

(SHEENA's eyes flicker to ROACH, who nods.)

IBIS: While she's gone, I'm leading this Rebellion.

ROACH: Until she comes back.

IBIS: So, Sheena. Can you take orders, or do we finish what the Legion started?

SHEENA: Is that a threat?

IBIS: It's your choice. Threats are a luxury we don't have time for.
Put the gun down.

(A long, tense moment. SHEENA puts the safety back on the gun and tucks it under her pillow.)

SHEENA: There. Happy?

IBIS: Not really.

SHEENA: Me neither. My brother used to say that's how compromises were supposed to work.

ROACH: Bit of a cynic, was he?

SHEENA: No. Not really.

(Pause. No one moves.)

IBIS: Tssa? What are you waiting for?

TSSA: Her consent.

SHEENA: I put the gun down, didn't I?

TSSA: That's not the same thing.

(SHEENA thaws, just slightly.)

SHEENA: Fine.

(TSSA approaches. SHEENA holds still, with effort. ROACH moves to IBIS.)

ROACH: *(Hushed)* That was a pretty strong reaction.

IBIS: *(Quietly)* And?

ROACH: Not something you'd expect from a Legion spy.

IBIS: It could be an act.

ROACH: Didn't look like one to me.

IBIS: ...No. But that's not proof.

ROACH: It's a start.

(A beat as both consider. SHEENA notices them.)

ROACH: *(Louder)* So. Sounds like the patrols still haven't found anything.

IBIS: Roach.

ROACH: It's not a secret.

IBIS: No. No sign of her.

SHEENA: It's been two weeks.

ROACH: There hasn't been any evidence that she's dead.

IBIS: She crashed in the middle of Lake Superior. What would we find?

ROACH: You can't just give up on her.

IBIS: I'm just trying to be realistic.

ROACH: You're talking about—

IBIS: I know who she is. Don't presume to tell me how to feel about what happened to her.

TSSA: *(Loudly, as if she's heard none of this.)* You're healing well. I expect you'll be back on your feet in a few days.

SHEENA: If I'm not executed as a goddamn spy before then, anyway.

IBIS: We have to be careful.

SHEENA: Yeah. I get it.

IBIS: Point that thing at one of us again, you won't leave this base alive. Spy or no spy. Understood?

(Pause)

SHEENA: Understood.

(IBIS *exits. Awkward silence.*)

SHEENA: *(To* ROACH) Question for you.

ROACH: *(With an effort to be casual)* Hit me.

SHEENA: Roach isn't exactly going to strike fear into the hearts of the Legion. Why'd you pick it?

ROACH: Because those bastards haven't managed to kill me yet.

(Transition. The past. SHEENA *watches* HSSIK *work until the Medic starts to clean up xyr supplies.)*

SHEENA: You're done? Already?

HSSIK: I've done all I can.

SHEENA: What does that mean?

(HSSIK *continues cleaning up.*)

SHEENA: Answer me, lizard!

(MICAH *stirs.*)

SHEENA: Micah! How d'you feel?

MICAH: Like I got run over by a truck. Maybe two.

(MICAH *prods at his side.*)

MICAH: Oh, holy *shit.*

SHEENA: What?

MICAH: It's gone.

SHEENA: What? Completely?

MICAH: There's a scar, maybe, but like it's months old.

SHEENA: How the hell?

MICAH: It's not even sore.

SHEENA: What did you do?

HSSIK: What you wanted me to. I fixed him. Can I go now?

SHEENA: Late for something?

HSSIK: No. I just don't enjoy being around a pair of homicidal humans.

MICAH: I hurt too much to be homicidal.

SHEENA: Doesn't sound like you fixed him.

HSSIK: I'm a Medic, not a miracle worker. I've stopped the bleeding, but his body was put through a lot of stress.

SHEENA: How long until he's back on his feet?

MICAH: I'm good to go. (*He tries to get up. He fails miserably.*) Ooh, never mind. Ow.

SHEENA: How long, lizard?

HSSIK: My *name* is Hssik.

SHEENA: How. Long.

HSSIK: How should I know? I'm not familiar with your species.

SHEENA: Ballpark it for me.

HSSIK: What?

SHEENA: Estimate.

HSSIK: Maybe a week?

SHEENA: Not good enough.

HSSIK: I've done all that I can.

SHEENA: I don't believe you.

MICAH: Easy, Sheena.

HSSIK: You said it yourself, I want to live. I did what you asked, and I would really like to go back to the Legion now—

SHEENA: No.

HSSIK: What more do you want?

(SHEENA *digs in her pack and comes up with a chain and padlock.*)

SHEENA: I want to make sure my brother survives. So you're staying until I'm sure.

MICAH: You just carry that around with you for a rainy day?

SHEENA: Figured it might come in handy. (*To* HSSIK) Over there.

(SHEENA *tethers* HSSIK *to a large piece of debris or other immovable object. She takes all of the Medic's possessions.*)

SHEENA: What, no weapon?

HSSIK: No.

SHEENA: Nothing up your sleeves?

HSSIK: No. Medics aren't allowed weapons.

SHEENA: Uh-huh.

HSSIK: How long are you intending to keep me here?

SHEENA: Until my brother walks out of here on his own two feet.

HSSIK: I told you, I don't know how long that will take.

SHEENA: Then I guess you'd better get comfy.

Scene 2

(The present. SHEENA, *alone in the makeshift medbay. She considers the door as the radio plays.)*

RADIO 1: —Legion activity is slowing down again. We should be able to resume normal operations soon, once the smoke in the air clears enough for us to track their ships. If anybody out there has any more information—

*(*SHEENA *makes a face, changes the station.)*

RADIO 2: —let me get this straight. Badger steals a ship from under the Legion's noses. Manages to stay away from them for over a week, broadcasting all the while. And y'all think she died just because she crashed into the lake? Please. That was just her exit strategy. She'll show back up when she's ready—

RADIO 3: —doesn't matter how good you are, or how many aliens you've killed. Everyone's luck has to run out sometime—

RADIO 4: —raid on Meridian the other day seems to have pissed them off a bit.

(As the radio continues, SHEENA *sits slowly up, favoring her wounded arm. It's more of a struggle than she wants it to be. She eyes the door, considering.)*

RADIO 4: They've been flying low over the trees, trying to find us—or flush us out from under cover, maybe— but we know this terrain better than they ever will.

They can look as long as they like, but they won't find us, and they won't scare us.

(SHEENA *has just put her feet on the ground to try and stand when the door opens.* TSSA *enters. She and* SHEENA *lock eyes.* SHEENA'*s hand is under her pillow, on the gun.*)

TSSA: Please. Pretend I'm not here.

SHEENA: Yeah. Right.

(TSSA *pointedly shuts the door and goes to the shelves.* SHEENA *watches her.*)

RADIO 4: They may have gotten Badger—though I'm not convinced, and if you knew her at all, neither are you—but as long as I'm alive, we'll keep the fire burning down here in the South. Croc out.

(*Static.* SHEENA *doesn't move.*)

TSSA: If you're planning to shoot your way out, you may want to wait until you can walk on your own.

SHEENA: Don't taunt me.

TSSA: Consider it my official medical advice.

SHEENA: You're no doctor.

TSSA: I'm the closest thing you've got.

(*A moment.* SHEENA *pulls her hand out from under the pillow and turns the radio off.*)

TSSA: Do you want anything for pain?

SHEENA: I'd rather keep my head clear.

TSSA: For when you shoot your way out?

SHEENA: Why bother? Not like I have anywhere else to go. (*Silence*) Why didn't Badger kill you?

TSSA: Ah, there it is.

SHEENA: I figured she of all people would've.

TSSA: She almost did.

SHEENA: You didn't answer my question.

TSSA: I haven't decided if I'm going to yet.

SHEENA: That's not suspicious at all.

TSSA: You're the newcomer here, not me. I don't owe you an answer. If anything, you owe me.

SHEENA: Gonna hold that over my head, huh?

TSSA: I suspect it's one of very few things keeping you from shooting me, so, for now? Yes.

SHEENA: I may owe you, but I don't trust you.

TSSA: You've made that very clear. *(Pause)* What happened to your eye? A wound like that should've killed you, but it was well healed when you arrived.

SHEENA: You think I'm gonna tell you that?

TSSA: Worth a shot.

SHEENA: Why even ask? Why do you care?

TSSA: Why shouldn't I?

SHEENA: I wouldn't care, if I was you.

TSSA: I wouldn't expect you to.

(Pause)

SHEENA: I was trying to protect someone.

TSSA: Did you succeed?

SHEENA: I don't know.

TSSA: That must be hard.

SHEENA: …Yeah.

(ROACH *enters.*)

ROACH: Sorry I'm late.

TSSA: Have a seat.

(ROACH *hops up to sit on one of the beds.* TSSA *starts rummaging in her cabinets.*)

ROACH: *(To* SHEENA*)* Good to see you on your feet.

SHEENA: Barely.

ROACH: Tssa taking good care of you?

*(*SHEENA *makes a noncommittal noise.)*

ROACH: Have you picked a moniker yet?

SHEENA: What?

ROACH: For the radio.

SHEENA: Hadn't really thought about it.

ROACH: Why not?

SHEENA: Well, I'm not sure yet that you're not gonna take me out in the backyard and shoot me.

ROACH: I'd say the odds are pretty good in your favor on that one.

SHEENA: Sounds like it's not your call to make.

ROACH: Yeah. Well.

(Silence. TSSA *comes over with a strange-looking device.)*

TSSA: *(To* ROACH*)* Ready?

ROACH: Ready.

*(*ROACH *presents their arm to* TSSA*, who clamps the device down on their forearm.)*

SHEENA: What is that thing doing?

ROACH: Taking a blood sample.

TSSA: This device can punch through a Brute's armor plating like—Roach, give me a phrase?

ROACH: A hot knife through butter.

TSSA: Sure.

SHEENA: What's it for? Are you sick?

ROACH: Kind of the opposite, actually.

SHEENA: What d'you mean?

(The door opens and IBIS *enters, rolling an unconscious and badly wounded Legion Soldier—*AWRLL*—on a cart or wheelchair.* AWRLL *is canine—bipedal, but only just. Her fur is matted with blood.)*

SHEENA: Holy shit.

IBIS: *(Out of breath)* Roach, help me.

ROACH: What did you do?

IBIS: Help me.

*(*IBIS *and* ROACH *manage to hoist the Soldier onto one of the open beds.* TSSA *makes no move to help.)*

IBIS: Well?

TSSA: You expect me to save her?

IBIS: That is what you do, isn't it?

TSSA: Why? *(Pause)* Say it. Why did you bring her here?

IBIS: This Soldier is from the battalion—

TSSA: Pack.

IBIS: Yes, fine, the *pack* that's been searching the banks of Superior for Badger. If any sign of her has been found, this Soldier should know.

TSSA: She won't tell you anything.

IBIS: Only one way to find out.

TSSA: I will not fix her just so you can take her apart.

IBIS: I didn't say anything about that.

SHEENA: You're going to torture her.

IBIS: Does that bother you?

SHEENA: Shouldn't it?

ROACH: Runs in the family, huh, Ibis?

IBIS: What?

ROACH: Remember? Badger got her hands on a Soldier once, too.

TSSA: I remember.

SHEENA: And?

(An uncomfortable pause)

IBIS: She got good information from it. Information that saved lives.

TSSA: I won't do this.

IBIS: And if I tell you it's an order?

TSSA: There are lines I will not cross.

(Beat. IBIS considers TSSA.)

IBIS: When you joined us—no. When Badger spared your life. You promised to trust her judgment when it came to the Legion.

TSSA: I have. You are not Badger.

IBIS: Badger's not here.

TSSA: I'm aware.

IBIS: So we can only rely on you when she's here, is that it?

SHEENA: That's bullshit.

IBIS: Excuse me?

ROACH: She's right. You wouldn't ask a human to compromise on the basis of a promise she made years ago.

IBIS: You're taking her side.

ROACH: If I have to.

IBIS: We need to know. Whether Badger is dead or alive, we need to know, because until we do—until we know who leads us—this Rebellion is paralyzed. I refuse to let this be her legacy. I will not let the

Rebellion die just because we couldn't make a decision and move on.

Please, Tssa. This could be my one chance to find out what happened to my daughter.

TSSA: If I do this, I want your word--

IBIS: I can't do that. I—we need to know, whatever it takes.

TSSA: If I can bend, so must you. Promise me that, even if you don't get the answers you want, you won't take it that far. Otherwise, I will let that Soldier die, no matter what it costs me.

(Pause)

IBIS: Fine. You have my word.

ROACH: And mine.

(IBIS gives ROACH a look, but TSSA is already moving to the bed.)

TSSA: *(To the room in general)* Could you get my equipment, please?

(Transition. The past. A day or so later. SHEENA is trying to help MICAH stand, with little success.)

MICAH: Put me down. Put me down!

SHEENA: Micah—

MICAH: Put me down or I'm gonna fall down.

(SHEENA helps MICAH down, then whirls on HSSIK.)

SHEENA: He's not getting better.

MICAH: I think I feel worse, actually.

SHEENA: What the hell did you do?

HSSIK: I did everything I could.

SHEENA: I'm hearing a 'but'.

HSSIK: What?

SHEENA: You did everything you could, <u>but</u>?

HSSIK: I don't know what you're talking about.

SHEENA: You start lying to me, you're not very useful anymore.

(Pause)

HSSIK: You need to take him to the Legion.

SHEENA: No fucking way—

HSSIK: His internal injuries were severe, and my medical kit—while far better than anything you'd have—is limited.

SHEENA: You said you'd fixed him.

HSSIK: I *said* I did everything I could. I don't know anything about human biology! There was every chance what I did was enough, but apparently it wasn't and now you need to take your brother to the Legion.

MICAH: Why would the Legion help me, anyway?

HSSIK: If you came in with me, I could make sure—

SHEENA: We kidnap you at gunpoint, and suddenly you're feeling helpful?

HSSIK: *You* kidnapped me. He did nothing but be in the wrong place at the wrong time.

MICAH: Thank you.

HSSIK: Besides, you said it yourself, I want to live. If helping him will ensure that, then that's what I'll do.

SHEENA: What's to stop you from changing your mind once you're back with the Legion?

HSSIK: I don't suppose my word would suffice?

(SHEENA snorts.)

MICAH: Say we believe you, and the Legion decides to cooperate and fix me up. What happens to Sheena?

(Pause)

SHEENA: I'm an enemy soldier. They kill me, right?

HSSIK: Maybe.

SHEENA: Definitely.

HSSIK: Not all captured soldiers are killed.

SHEENA: I bet. I'm sure some are interrogated first. Or maybe experimented on. Brainwashed, even.

HSSIK: We don't brainwash.

SHEENA: Sure you don't.
Micah?

MICAH: Maybe I can still turn it around.

SHEENA: You sure?

MICAH: Yeah. No Legion.

SHEENA: Okay.

HSSIK: You're making a mistake.

SHEENA: Shut up.

MICAH: What now?

SHEENA: If we're staying, we're going to need more food. I'll head out, see what I can find.

(SHEENA rummages in her pack and comes up with food, water, a handheld radio, and a pistol. She brings all of this to MICAH.)

SHEENA: Signal's not great under here, but this should work well enough. If something goes wrong, call.

MICAH: Got it.

(SHEENA hands MICAH the gun.)

MICAH: Sheena—

SHEENA: Take it. I don't want to leave you defenseless.

MICAH: I have no idea how to use this.

SHEENA: Safety's here. Then just point the hole at the bad guy and shoot.

MICAH: That easy, huh?

SHEENA: More or less. Try to keep your thumb down so it doesn't get hit by the slide when you fire.

MICAH: Right.

SHEENA: This part. See?

MICAH: Just go, okay? The sooner you go, the sooner you come back and maybe I don't have to use this thing.

SHEENA: Fine.

(SHEENA *stands and starts for the door, but stops to look at* HSSIK *before exiting.*)

SHEENA: Remember. He dies, you die.

HSSIK: I remember, human.

(SHEENA *exits. Transition: the present.* TSSA *finishes patching up the Soldier.*)

IBIS: Well?

TSSA: She'll survive.

IBIS: How long before she wakes up?

TSSA: Maybe twelve hours? I've never tried human sedative on a Soldier before.

ROACH: What I want to know is how the hell did she get here? There shouldn't be Legion Soldiers anywhere near here.

IBIS: Easy, Roach. It was my idea.

TSSA: What?

IBIS: I told the patrols: <u>if</u> they saw an opportunity, to take one of the Soldiers from the packs around the lake.

TSSA: So you planned this. You deliberately kidnapped—

IBIS: Would you rather the Legion had found us? *(Brief pause)* I thought not.

ROACH: They still might. They could follow the Soldier's trail back to the base. You know how good their Trackers are.

IBIS: The patrols know how to cover their tracks.

ROACH: You're sure about that? Even with a wounded Soldier bleeding everywhere? *(Pause)* You put this entire base at risk.

IBIS: I saw an opportunity, and I took it. I won't apologize for that.

ROACH: And if it gets us all killed?

IBIS: Then you can tell my corpse you told me so. I'll up the guard rotation outside and tell them to keep their eyes out. Alright?

ROACH: Fine.

IBIS: We'll need restraints for the Soldier, as well.

ROACH: I'll watch her in the meantime.

IBIS: Thank you, Tssa.

TSSA: Just remember what you promised.

IBIS: I do.

Scene 3

(The past. The light lancing through the ceiling has faded— it's night. MICAH lies in the rubble, fiddling with the walkie-talkie as he tries to get a signal. HSSIK sits slumped against the wall, eyes open but unmoving.)

(Garbled noises from the radio)

MICAH: Come on, come on.

RADIO 1: —fight, fight! As long as you're still alive, you can still fight. And as long as I'm breathing, I'll be right here with you on the airwaves, reminding you that you're not alone. I'm here with you, and we're gonna show the Legion just who they're fucking with—

RADIO 2: —civilians in small towns are advised to stay in their homes. Repeat, stay in your homes. If the Legion comes, do not fight them. Reports suggest that you will be rounded up and transported to an unknown location. If you resist, you will die. *(The radio dies in a burst of static.)*

MICAH: Damnit.

(MICAH can't get the signal back. He puts the radio aside.)

MICAH: Hey. Hey! *(No response)* Hey, lizard! *(Nothing)* What'd you say before—Hss...Hissik?

(A flicker.)

MICAH: Hmm.

(MICAH grabs a rock from nearby and chucks it into the wall near HSSIK. HSSIK raises xyr head slowly, groggy.)

MICAH: You're freaking me out.

HSSIK: *(Slowly)* Have to...conserve energy.

MICAH: Why?

HSSIK: Cold-blooded.

MICAH: Oh. I get it. *(Pause)* Hang on. *(He pulls SHEENA's jacket out from underneath him.)* Here.

(MICAH chucks it at HSSIK.)

HSSIK: What?

MICAH: I've been lying on it all day. It's warm.

(HSSIK *blinks at the jacket, then at* MICAH. *Then xe wraps it around xyr shoulders, huddling down into it in obvious relief.*)

MICAH: Better?

HSSIK: Yes.
Thank you.

MICAH: Don't mention it. *(Pause)* Tell me your name again? Hissik?

HSSIK: Hssik. One syllable.

MICAH: Hssik.

HSSIK: Yes. And you're Micah. That's a type of rock, right?

MICAH: I just liked the sound of it.

HSSIK: You chose your own name?

MICAH: I'm a bit of an outlier that way. Most people stick with the one their parents give them. Does your name mean anything?

HSSIK: No. It's just a name.

(HSSIK *pulls the jacket closer, huddling down. Xe shifts around.*)

MICAH: What are you doing?

HSSIK: Finding a more comfortable position. The heat is already starting to fade.

MICAH: Oh. *(Pause)* Can you reach me?

HSSIK: Is something wrong?

MICAH: Come here.

HSSIK: Why?

MICAH: I've got body heat to spare.

(HSSIK *hesitates.*)

MICAH: I won't make it weird, I promise. I just really don't want to be alone down here all night.

(Another pause. Slowly, HSSIK gets up and makes xyr way to MICAH. The tether is just long enough to allow it. Xe eventually settles into the rubble next to MICAH.)

MICAH: Better?

HSSIK: Yes. If your sister sees—

MICAH: I'll handle it.

HSSIK: I have my doubts that she'd listen.

MICAH: Let's just say stubborn runs in the family.

HSSIK: I believe you.

(Silence. It's weird, but HSSIK and MICAH are both pretending it's not. The sound of Legion ships in the distance.)

MICAH: You called yourself a Medic, before.

HSSIK: Yes?

MICAH: What does that mean, exactly? Like, is that your job, or your title, or…?

HSSIK: It is what I am.

MICAH: Okayyy…

HSSIK: As you are a human, I am a Medic.

MICAH: That's the name of your species?

HSSIK: It's what we are called, yes. And also what we do.

MICAH: All of you have the same job?

HSSIK: More or less.

MICAH: That's. Really fucking weird.

HSSIK: How so? We are well suited for it.

MICAH: I guess. I just—y'know, most humans don't even do the same job their whole lives. I can't imagine an entire species all doing the same thing. And all the species in the Legion are like that?

HSSIK: Yes.

MICAH: Huh. *(Pause)* Do you enjoy it?

HSSIK: What?

MICAH: Being a Medic. I assume that means you help people? Keep them from dying?

HSSIK: Among other things.

MICAH: So?

HSSIK: Does it matter?

MICAH: I think it does.

(Pause)

HSSIK: You're going to die, you know.

MICAH: What?

HSSIK: If you stay here in this pit, you will die.

MICAH: You think so, huh?

HSSIK: It's not what I think, it's what I know.

MICAH: I'm tougher than I look.

HSSIK: It's not about 'tough'. Stupid, thickheaded human. You don't understand. Maybe you *won't*. Maybe you're too stubborn to face your own mortality, so you deny it. Is that it?

MICAH: Oh, I am intimately aware of my own mortality.

HSSIK: Really.

MICAH: Seeing your family get vaporized in front of you will do that.

HSSIK: Then why won't you listen? Do you think I'm lying? If I were willing to lie, I would have told your

sister you were healed. Maybe she would've let me go,
and I could be finished with all this.

MICAH: Look, you said yourself you don't know
human biology. What makes you so sure I'm a goner?

HSSIK: I've seen wounds like yours before. I know what
made them.

MICAH: I thought weapons weren't a Medic thing.

HSSIK: They aren't. Usually.

MICAH: What's different about this one? *(Silence)*
Hssik?

HSSIK: I've said too much already. If Command finds
out I told a human—

MICAH: I'm doomed, remember? Who am I gonna tell?

HSSIK: Your sister.

MICAH: And who's she gonna tell? We're all alone
here. Nobody to spill the beans to.

HSSIK: Beans?

MICAH: Skip it.
Come on. If I'm gonna die, don't I at least deserve to
know what killed me?

(Pause)

HSSIK: It was supposed to be a medicine. It was never
supposed to hurt anyone.

MICAH: But.

HSSIK: It was too strong. The same mechanism as our
healing spray, but exponentially more powerful. It
doesn't just regenerate cells, it causes them to grow out
of control.

MICAH: That's fucked up.

HSSIK: As I said, it was an accident. Given time, we
could have found a way to regulate it. But Command

saw the potential in a weapon like that, that took its time to kill. A slow death is so much more frightening than a quick one. And it gives the Legion a chance to play hero, should they choose to do so.

MICAH: Just how many species have you seen them take over?

HSSIK: Personally? Yours is the first.

MICAH: But your species.

HSSIK: We were the fifth to "join" the Legion. There are eleven. Do the math.

MICAH: But you didn't have the weapon back then, right? When you first 'joined'?

HSSIK: No.

(Pause)

MICAH: What if people who've been hit with this weapon don't go to the Legion?

HSSIK: We don't have a single recorded case of someone surviving without Legion intervention.

MICAH: How does that not wipe out entire species?

HSSIK: It's not contagious beyond the first exposure.

MICAH: So Sheena doesn't have it.

HSSIK: She wasn't here when…?

MICAH: No. She got here a couple of days ago. Found me bleeding out just outside of town.

HSSIK: Then no. Besides, she would be showing signs by now.

MICAH: Good. Good.

HSSIK: So you see?

MICAH: Why don't you Medics carry the antidote?

HSSIK: It would defeat the purpose. Command controls the antidote, just as they control the weapon.

MICAH: They don't much like to share, do they?

(HSSIK *laughs.*)

HSSIK: No. No, I don't think sharing is in their vocabulary.

MICAH: I get the feeling you don't like them much. (*Pause*) Hssik?

HSSIK: You're...not incorrect.

MICAH: Why go back, then?

HSSIK: I don't think I'm going anywhere at the moment.

MICAH: But after...this. Why go back?

HSSIK: I don't see any other choice.

MICAH: Maybe you're not looking hard enough.

HSSIK: Maybe.
So. Will you go to the Legion?

MICAH: I...don't know.

HSSIK: You have no other choice.

MICAH: I don't want to leave my sister behind. She's all I have left.

HSSIK: Bring her with us. She would go, if you asked her.

MICAH: I won't ask her.

HSSIK: Why not?

MICAH: Because you're right. She'd go, if I asked her to, and she'd die. Maybe not as quickly as if she were fighting the Legion outright, but it would kill her, eventually.

HSSIK: How do you know that?

MICAH: Because I know my sister. She's never known when—or how—to stop. Either she'd piss off the Legion and get herself executed, or she'd die slowly by inches, because surrendering isn't in <u>her</u> vocabulary.

HSSIK: I don't understand.

MICAH: It's okay. You don't have to. The point is, if I go to the Legion, I'm either killing my sister, or leaving her behind.

HSSIK: And if you don't go, you die.

MICAH: Talk about a rock and a hard place.

HSSIK: What?

MICAH: Never mind.

(*Silence.* MICAH *goes back to the radio. Transition: the present.* SHEENA *is cleaning her pistol.* AWRLL *sleeps in the other bed, now restrained.* ROACH *sits nearby.*)

ROACH: Any progress on the name front?

SHEENA: What?

ROACH: Your name. Moniker. Callsign. Whatever you want to call it.

SHEENA: Wasn't really planning on using one.

ROACH: Going without is a good way to get any family you've got left in trouble.

SHEENA: Yeah, well. Like I said.

ROACH: You don't have anyone?

SHEENA: No.

ROACH: Still—

SHEENA: The Legion's taken everything else from me. You want me to let them take my name, too?

ROACH: It's not like that.

SHEENA: It kind of is.

ROACH: Just…give it some thought. Make sure there really isn't anybody out there you might still want to protect.

SHEENA: Still trying to get me to talk, huh?

ROACH: Is it working?

SHEENA: Not so much. *(Pause)* What makes you so sure she's not dead? Badger, I mean.

ROACH: Changing the subject, huh?

SHEENA: Is it working?

ROACH: I've seen Badger do a lot of crazy things. This wouldn't be the craziest.

SHEENA: What would be?

ROACH: Most people would say letting Tssa live. Half the base thought Badger had gone off the deep end when she told us.

SHEENA: Why did she?

ROACH: You'd have to ask Tssa.

SHEENA: Since Badger's not here.

ROACH: Well. She was never really the type for explaining herself anyway, to be honest. Once she made a decision, it was a done deal.

SHEENA: That tracks.

ROACH: We trusted her.

SHEENA: I wish I'd gotten here sooner. Gotten to meet her.

ROACH: You might, still.

SHEENA: Right.
Doesn't seem like Ibis agrees with you.

ROACH: No. It's hard, not knowing.

SHEENA: Tell me about it.

(AWRLL *stirs.* SHEENA *and* ROACH *both freeze.* SHEENA *puts her gun back together.*)

ROACH: The hell? It's only been a couple of hours.

SHEENA: Guess your lizard isn't as good as she thinks she is.

ROACH: I'd better get the others. You good here?

SHEENA: She's restrained. I'll be fine.

ROACH: It's not really you I'm worried about.

(ROACH *looks at* SHEENA's *gun.*)

SHEENA: I'm a soldier, not a murderer.

(*A moment.* ROACH *exits.*)

AWRLL: It *reeks* of humans in here.

SHEENA: Funny story.

(AWRLL *finally opens her eyes.*)

SHEENA: Howdy.

AWRLL: The Rebellion.

SHEENA: Got it in one.

AWRLL: I'll tell you nothing. I'll die before I spill Legion secrets.

SHEENA: Slow down, tiger.

AWRLL: You should kill me now.

SHEENA: Not gonna happen.

AWRLL: Then whatever happens next is on your head.

(IBIS, ROACH, *and* TSSA *enter.* AWRLL's *eyes immediately focus on* TSSA.)

AWRLL: Traitor.

TSSA: Just once, I wish someone was happy to see me.

AWRLL: Turncoat. Deserter.

IBIS: We have a few questions to ask you.

AWRLL: What did they promise to turn you away from the Legion?

IBIS: Soldier.

AWRLL: Are you so tired of your place in the world that you would turn to humans?

IBIS: Tssa. I think you should go.

TSSA: What?

IBIS: You're a distraction. I think it's best you wait outside.

AWRLL: Is it better, taking orders from them? From a species so far beneath us?

(Pause)

TSSA: I'm staying.

IBIS: Roach—

ROACH: She has a right to be here.

(IBIS *takes a deep breath, and turns back to* AWRLL.)

IBIS: Soldier.

AWRLL: Human.

IBIS: Are you comfortable?

AWRLL: Kill me. Get it over with.

IBIS: That would be a great deal of wasted effort.

AWRLL: So will your questions.

IBIS: We'll see.

AWRLL: Then stop wasting my time. Ask, so I can be done with this.

IBIS: Fine. Have you found any sign of Badger?

(Pause)

AWRLL: That's it?

IBIS: Yes.

AWRLL: I expected questions about Legion movements, the strength and number of our forces.

IBIS: If you'd like to share that, feel free.

AWRLL: No.

IBIS: All I want to know is, have you found her? A scent, a trace, anything that suggests she might not have drowned in that lake?

(AWRLL *considers.*)

AWRLL: I will tell you nothing.

IBIS: Why not? What harm would it do?

AWRLL: We do not cooperate with humans.

IBIS: What harm would it do?

AWRLL: I do not cooperate with humans.

(Pause)

IBIS: What would it take?

AWRLL: You have nothing I want.

IBIS: What about your freedom? What is that worth to you?

AWRLL: I'm not stupid, human. Letting me live would be too much of a risk.

IBIS: That's true. But there are many ways to die.

TSSA: Ibis.

AWRLL: Hurt me if you must. I will not break the Code.

IBIS: I didn't say anything about hurting you.

AWRLL: You didn't have to.

IBIS: I'm not going to hurt you.

AWRLL: Then your threats mean nothing.

IBIS: Are you sure about that?

AWRLL: Humans. Always talking around the point. Tell me, then—if I don't give you the answer you want, what will you do?

IBIS: Nothing.

(A confused pause)

AWRLL: Nothing?

IBIS: Nothing. I don't have to do anything to you, Soldier. I've already done the only thing that matters. I've taken you away from your pack.

AWRLL: I have been away from them before.

IBIS: But for how long? You know as well as I do what's going to happen. How long do you think it'll take, Tssa?

TSSA: Ibis.

IBIS: A week? Two?

AWRLL: *(To* TSSA*)* You told them?

TSSA: I didn't—

IBIS: She didn't have to. You aren't the first Soldier we've taken, and if you don't tell me what I want to know, you won't be the last.

AWRLL: *(To* TSSA*)* Not just a traitor, then. A monster.

TSSA: I'm not—

AWRLL: You must be, to help them do this.

TSSA:	SHEENA:
You think I wanted this?	Hold the fuck up—

AWRLL:	IBIS:
They couldn't do it without you.	You stay out of this.

TSSA:	SHEENA:
I never wanted—	This isn;t right and you know it.

AWRLL:
It doesn't matter what
you want, it matters
what you do. If the
Legion knew what you'd
done, they'd eradicate
your entire species.

IBIS:
What I know is that we
need answers. I don't know
or care what you thought
this Rebellion would be,
but someone has to make
the hard decisions here.

ROACH: *(Louder than we've ever heard them before)*
ENOUGH. *(Silence)* We have to be better than this.
This can't be who we are. Torture? Kidnapping enemy
soldiers? How does that not make us just as bad as
they are?

IBIS: You didn't argue it last time.

ROACH: That was then.

IBIS: What else am I supposed to do, Roach? We need
to know.

ROACH: No, we don't.
You're right about one thing. We can't keep waiting for
Badger to come back and make all the decisions for us.

IBIS: Exactly. Which is why I—

ROACH: And who gave you the right? No one gave you
the right to decide for all of us. We follow Badger, not
you. If she's gone, then we'll figure out where to go
next together. All of us.

AWRLL: Pretty words, human.

IBIS: We shouldn't be having this conversation here.

ROACH: Fine. Badger's room, five minutes.

IBIS: Fine.

(Both exit. TSSA *stares after them, fists clenched.)*

AWRLL: Poor little Medic. At least in the Legion you
knew your place. It wasn't personal.

SHEENA: Tssa.

TSSA: What?

SHEENA: You have something to say?

TSSA: Yes.

SHEENA: Then go say it. What the hell are you waiting for?

(TSSA *stares at her for a long moment. Then exits, leaving* AWRLL *and* SHEENA *alone.*)

AWRLL: Do it.

SHEENA: Fuck you. I'm a soldier, not a murderer.

AWRLL: What's the difference? A Soldier is a killer. They are the same thing. What difference does it make where and when the killing happens?

SHEENA: This isn't a battlefield.

AWRLL: But I am your enemy.

SHEENA: And you want me to kill you. So I'd be doing you a favor.

AWRLL: That's not why you won't.

(*Pause*)

SHEENA: No. It's not.

Scene 4

(*The present.* SHEENA *paces painfully back and forth.* AWRLL *dozes fitfully in and out. The radio plays.*)

RADIO 1: —what stations we still have access to seem to suggest that there has been significant ecological improvement since the Legion arrived. Whether this is a deliberate effort on their part, or just the result of a lack of human industry, it's difficult to say—

(SHEENA *makes a face and turns to a different channel.*)

RADIO 2: —northern bank of Superior is—or was—in Canada, right? Maybe this whole thing was just a cover for her to finally break past the border, find out what's going on out there. Just wait—I bet she comes back in a few weeks with a bunch of reinforcements—

RADIO 3: —the rest left early yesterday morning. They should be back at base around midnight, if someone can bring them a ride across Erie. I'll stay out here, hold down the fort while you do what you need to do.

RADIO 4: (IBIS) Thank you. Have there been any other changes?

RADIO 3: There was some activity around the spot where we grabbed that Soldier, but otherwise? No. Sorry. If something happens, you'll be the first to know. I promise.

(SHEENA *pauses, watching the radio as it dissolves into static. A moment.* ROACH *enters.*)

SHEENA: Just you this time?

ROACH: Just me. Disappointed?

SHEENA: Nah. Where's the lizard?

ROACH: I'd appreciate it if you didn't call her that.

(*Pause*)

SHEENA: Yeah. Okay.

ROACH: She's getting some air.

SHEENA: Is that…never mind.

ROACH: No, what?

SHEENA: Is that safe?

ROACH: Medics are pretty hard to track, apparently. Not as smelly as us mammals are.

SHEENA: That's not exactly what I meant.

ROACH: I know. But it's what matters.

SHEENA: …Right.

ROACH: It's tough for her here. A lot of people don't agree with what Badger did, letting her live.

SHEENA: I take it you're not one of those people.

ROACH: She's proven herself a half dozen times over. More than most of us. But it'll never be enough for some.

SHEENA: Can you blame them?

ROACH: Kind of, yeah. Badger figured it out, didn't she?

SHEENA: Still can't quite believe that. Coming from someone whose motto was "as long as you're breathing, you can still fight".

ROACH: Ah. A classic.

(Pause)

SHEENA: You didn't answer me before.

ROACH: About what?

SHEENA: The craziest thing Badger's ever done. In your opinion.

ROACH: Hmm.
I'd have to go with…she took a team to try and snatch some medical equipment—some for Tssa, some to hand over to the techs to take apart. Keep in mind some of the things they were after were probably fifty pounds or more of solid metal. Turns out the Legion doesn't like to share. There were at least a dozen Soldier packs after them, not to mention the Trackers and the eyes overhead—*and* it was the middle of winter, with fresh snow all over the ground leaving tracks.

SHEENA: Shit.

ROACH: And not only did she get everyone out alive and back to base—she managed to bring back all the loot, too. The Aurora techs just about threw her a party.
What's your favorite Badger story?

SHEENA: That's easy. Imitating a Legionnaire. Rest of the team dead, pinned down on all sides, and she takes down the first pack she sees—by herself, which is already fucking nuts—picks up a communicator off a dead Soldier and somehow convinces them to look the other way long enough to get the hell out of dodge.

ROACH: I think even she couldn't believe that worked.

SHEENA: I always wanted to ask her…well. I guess it doesn't matter, does it?
I should've come sooner.

ROACH: Hmm?

SHEENA: To join up. I shouldn't have waited so long.

ROACH: Then why did you?

(Pause)

SHEENA: I was a soldier when the Legion hit. In training, technically. Never actually made it to the front lines, in the end, but I did get a front row seat to the goddamn alien apocalypse. We threw everything we had at them and it didn't even slow them down. Then I threw everything I had into protecting my family, and…same fucking thing. There wasn't a Rebellion yet, then. I didn't think there was any fight left. But once I started listening to the radio, to Badger and the others…I knew it wasn't over. Just took me a little too long to realize it.

ROACH: Not quite how you imagined it would be, huh?

SHEENA: No.

ROACH: Sorry to disappoint.

SHEENA: That's not what I meant. It's hard to believe, is all. That after hearing her every night for three years, after all the bugnuts shit she survived, that she's just… gone.
I guess I didn't really know her, but…I'm getting really fucking tired of losing people.

ROACH: I know the feeling.

SHEENA: Yeah. I bet. (Pause) So. I heard Ibis, calling in the troops. What's that about?

ROACH: Well, after our little talk yesterday, about the only thing we really agreed on was that we couldn't keep dragging this out.

SHEENA: So you're choosing a new leader.

ROACH: Looks that way.

SHEENA: How's that gonna work? You versus Ibis in a battle to the death?

ROACH: Ha. That'd be more exciting, maybe, but no. If I had my way, no one would have to fill Badger's shoes.

SHEENA: What do you mean?

ROACH: Badger could be. Stubborn.

SHEENA: No shit.

ROACH: Not always in a good way. It's hard to describe if you didn't know her. She wasn't all that intimidating, at least at first, but… It was like, once she said something was true, or was going to happen, there was no debating it. Reality itself bent to match what she said. Like with the Legionnaires.
But. It got us into trouble, sometimes. There's a lot of good minds in this base, and none of us can be good at everything.

SHEENA: You'd rather lead by committee, huh?

ROACH: Maybe. But Ibis made a good point—in a war, someone has to be able to make fast decisions. So.

SHEENA: So?

ROACH: So, we're going to figure it out at the meeting. Most likely we'll end up with one person stepping up, but who knows.

SHEENA: Sounds very kumbaya.

ROACH: There are worse things to be.

(Pause. AWRLL *stirs.)*

AWRLL: Kill me, human.

ROACH: Sorry. No can do.

AWRLL: Then leave me alone.

ROACH: She say anything before I came in?

SHEENA: No. She's been pretty out of it.

ROACH: Shame.

SHEENA: That's it? You seemed pretty against it, before.

ROACH: It's not my call. Yet, anyway.
At least it'll be over soon.

(Transition. The past. HSSIK *is still next to* MICAH *in the rubble. Both are dozing. Radio static. The drone of Legion ships, growing slowly louder.* SHEENA *runs into the room, a bag of supplies over her shoulder. She skids to a stop at the sight of the two.)*

SHEENA: What the fuck?

MICAH: *(Groggy)* Hey, you're back!

SHEENA: *(Drawing her gun)* Get away from him, lizard.

MICAH: Woah, woah, woah.

HSSIK: Easy, human—

SHEENA: Five seconds. Five, four—

MICAH: Sheena, stop!

SHEENA: —three, two—

HSSIK: I was just trying to—

SHEENA: —one, zero. Time's up.

(SHEENA *raises the gun.* MICAH *clumsily leans in front of* HSSIK, *blocking the shot.)*

MICAH: Stop it!

SHEENA: What the hell, Micah?

MICAH: Xe's cold blooded. Xe was passing out over there.

SHEENA: So?

HSSIK: If I am unconscious, I can't help your brother.

SHEENA: I wasn't talking to you.

MICAH: Sheena. Xe's right, and you know it.

SHEENA: Always so fucking softhearted.

MICAH: Maybe I'm tired of people dying today.

SHEENA: "People."

MICAH: Yeah. People. If it walks like a people and quacks like a people...

SHEENA/HSSIK: *(Simultaneous)* What?

MICAH: Never mind.

SHEENA: I still don't like it.

MICAH: You don't have to.

(Pause. SHEENA *stomps over and moves the gun she gave* MICAH *out of* HSSIK's *reach, beyond the reach of the tether. The drone overhead is close.)*

SHEENA: At least keep this out of xyr reach.

MICAH: Fine. Happy?

SHEENA: No.

MICAH: Me neither. So it's a good compromise.

SHEENA: Oh, shove it.

(*The drone is nearly upon them.*)

HSSIK: Were you followed?

SHEENA: What?

HSSIK: The ships. They're close.

(*Pause*)

SHEENA: Fuck, you're right. You didn't signal them, did you?

HSSIK: With what, exactly?

MICAH: No time to argue.

SHEENA: Yeah, fine. I'll draw them off.
Remember, Medic?

HSSIK: He dies, I die.

SHEENA: Now you're catching on.
Micah, for the love of Christ, be careful.

MICAH: You, too.

(SHEENA *runs out. Over the next chunk of dialogue, the drone slowly fades back into the distance.*)

MICAH: See? Told you I'd handle it.

HSSIK: She is going to kill me, eventually.

MICAH: Give her a break. Our whole world just got blown to pieces.

HSSIK: Are all humans so prone to exaggeration?

MICAH: Huh?

HSSIK: It was hardly your whole world. Some chose to let us help.

MICAH: Is that what you call it.

HSSIK: That's all the Legion wants. To help.

MICAH: And how exactly does blowing my town to smithereens help?

HSSIK: You refuse to be helped.

MICAH: We have a right to.

HSSIK: Do you?

MICAH: Yes.

HSSIK: And where exactly has that gotten you?

MICAH: You expect me to believe that if we'd just given up, let you "help" us, it would've been all sunshine and kittens?

HSSIK: Kittens?
You know what? Never mind. (*Pause*) What was it like before?

MICAH: Before the Legion came?

HSSIK: Yes. Was your world falling apart, as Command said?

MICAH: I mean. Yeah, kind of.

HSSIK: Kind of?

MICAH: Day to day, everything was mostly fine. For a lot of people, anyway.

HSSIK: But not all.

MICAH: No. And in the long run… We knew we were ruining the world. Some people pretended not to, but we knew.

HSSIK: Why didn't you stop it? Not you alone, obviously, but your species?

MICAH: I wish I knew.

HSSIK: So the Legion did save this planet.

MICAH: We might've done it on our own, eventually. But yeah, I guess so. (*Pause*) Okay. Fine. What would have happened?

HSSIK: What?

MICAH: If we'd said yes. What would the Legion have done?

HSSIK: Does it really matter? That's not the world you're living in.

MICAH: Tell me. Please.

HSSIK: There would have been an adjustment period, of course. But in the end, you'd be better off.

MICAH: How so?

HSSIK: The Legion stops species from destroying themselves. Look at the Trackers. They nearly drove themselves to extinction. You said yourself, you were well on your way to following them, and taking your planet with you.

MICAH: What is a Tracker?

HSSIK: It's not important. The point is, with the Legion there to steer you away from your more self-destructive impulses, humanity would thrive.

MICAH: You really believe that?

HSSIK: It's worked before.

MICAH: I don't know. Stubborn and independent is kind of humanity's thing.

HSSIK: Perhaps you could have improved the Legion, just as it improved you.

MICAH: Guess we'll never know.

(Pause)

HSSIK: What were you then? Before we came.

MICAH: What do you mean?

HSSIK: I am a Medic. Your sister is obviously a soldier.

MICAH: I don't think she technically made it out of Basic yet, but yeah.

HSSIK: So what were you?

MICAH: Does it matter? That's over now.

HSSIK: Perhaps not. But I'd still like to know, if you're willing to tell me.

(Pause)

MICAH: I worked at a community center. It's, uh, it's like a building where people gather and take classes, sometimes there's childcare, sometimes there's a gym for people to exercise in, that kind of thing. I'd always thought I'd be a teacher, but uh…it didn't work out. I moved back home, ended up taking a job at Gateway Community Center. Not the most creative name, but the Y I applied to first made it pretty clear I wasn't welcome.

HSSIK: Why?

MICAH: Long story. Anyway, I just kind of took it because I couldn't think what else to do, but I ended up really enjoying it. Seeing all the people coming through, hearing kids laughing in the hallways…it was nice.

HSSIK: It sounds nice.

MICAH: I thought my parents would be disappointed, but they were just—they were just happy that I was happy.

(Pause)

HSSIK: I'm sorry, Micah. About your parents. What you've lost.

MICAH: It's not your fault.

HSSIK: Even so.

MICAH: …Thanks.

(Transition. The present)

ROACH: Well. If you'll excuse me, I'd better go help set up for the meeting. You good here?

SHEENA: Yeah. I'm good.

(ROACH *exits.* AWRLL *rouses a bit.*)

AWRLL: You're soft.

SHEENA: Something to say?

AWRLL: Your whole species. Soft.

SHEENA: We're putting up a pretty good fight.

AWRLL: Only the weak lead by consensus.

SHEENA: Your way is better, I'm sure.

AWRLL: The strong lead. It is their right.

SHEENA: For someone so obsessed with strength, you're sure tanking fast.

AWRLL: We are not meant to stand alone.

SHEENA: Seems like a weakness to me.

AWRLL: Perhaps. But our strength is in each other. And we are so strong, together. Surely you know this. Your species is weak, but you are stronger in packs.

SHEENA: Doesn't mean we need them.

AWRLL: Don't you?

SHEENA: I'm doing just fine without one.

AWRLL: You are new here.

SHEENA: Fucking Sherlock Holmes, aren't you?

AWRLL: Why would you come here, if not to join the pack?

SHEENA: To fight.

AWRLL: Why? You must know you can't win.

SHEENA: We'll see.

AWRLL: Tactically, you have no chance. We have the skies. We have the numbers. We have most of your population corralled like the sheep you are. Even one-on-one, you are no match for us.

SHEENA: Wanna bet?

AWRLL: Taking me down—wounded, starving of my Pack—would prove nothing.

SHEENA: I've killed plenty of you fuckers.

AWRLL: And yet we're still winning. We will always be winning. Why fight it? It's foolish. What are you fighting *for*?

SHEENA: Doesn't matter. I'll fight you til my dying day. I'd fight you if I was the last human alive.

AWRLL: Why?

SHEENA: Because someone has to.

Scene 5

(The medbay. The radio is on, but the signal is garbled, the static so loud that only a few words make it through. SHEENA is pacing again, moving more smoothly now. AWRLL isn't looking good.)

RADIO 1: —heard that Badger's crew is—a new leader tonight. Sorry to hear that. Just wanted—we're mourning her, too, but—having you back in the fight. Croc out.

(The radio dissolves fully into static. AWRLL groans, long and low and pained.)

AWRLL: Please.

(SHEENA doesn't respond.)

AWRLL: At least…

(Pause)

SHEENA: At least what?

AWRLL: The static. Hurts.

(SHEENA *considers. She turns the radio off.*)

SHEENA: Better?

(*No response*)

SHEENA: God.

(SHEENA *looks at* AWRLL *for a long moment. She goes to the bed, puts her hand under the pillow as if to check the gun is still there.* TSSA *enters. A still, slightly awkward moment.*)

TSSA: How is she doing?

(AWRLL *convulses. She chokes, retches, twists as much as her restraints will allow.* TSSA *hurries to the bed, eases her back once the spell passes.*)

AWRLL: (*Breathless*) If you have ever felt loyalty to the Legion...

TSSA: Not in a long time.

AWRLL: I will not beg you, traitor. And you have no honor left to appeal to.

(*She turns away and, a moment later, seems to have passed out again.*)

SHEENA: How much longer will this take?

TSSA: A couple of days, at most.

SHEENA: What's doing this?

TSSA: I suppose there's no reason you would know. It's withdrawal.

SHEENA: From what?

TSSA: Her pack. Soldiers bond fiercely with the other members of their pack. They become stronger together, in a literal, biological way. But when you take that away from them...

SHEENA: This.

TSSA: They waste away. They can't survive alone.

SHEENA: Will the rest of her pack die, too?

TSSA: No. They have each other, still.

SHEENA: Will they replace her?

TSSA: No.

(A moment. SHEENA *watches* TSSA *tend to* AWRLL.*)*

SHEENA: Why did you leave the Legion?

TSSA: You believe me now?

SHEENA: Call it morbid curiosity.

TSSA: We all have to do what we think is right.

SHEENA: That's not an answer.

TSSA: I didn't believe in the Legion anymore.

SHEENA: That's it?

TSSA: Isn't that enough? Why would I stay if I didn't believe?

SHEENA: I dunno. Inertia? Fear?

TSSA: I've lived long enough.

SHEENA: And you believe in the Rebellion? That it has a chance to win?

TSSA: Do you?

SHEENA: Why else would I come all this way?

TSSA: Inertia? Or hope, perhaps. I hear you humans like that sort of thing.

SHEENA: I came to kick some alien ass. Make them pay.

TSSA: Revenge.

SHEENA: Sure.

TSSA: For your world?

SHEENA: Well, yeah. And for my brother.

(Transition: the past. SHEENA *enters, looking a bit ragged from the chase. She crouches near* MICAH *to dig through the supplies.* HSSIK *moves away, back towards the rock xe is tethered to.)*

SHEENA: How are you feeling?

MICAH: Like shit. How's it look out there?

SHEENA: Like shit.

MICAH: Sounds like things have calmed down a bit.

SHEENA: Some. There's nobody left to fight back, but the Legion's still hanging around. Probably looking for the lizard.

HSSIK: Most likely.

MICAH: Do we need to move?

SHEENA: We'll be fine. Even if we weren't, you're in no shape to go anywhere.

MICAH: About that…

SHEENA: What?

MICAH: *(To* HSSIK*)* You can probably explain it better.

SHEENA: Explain what?

(A pause)

HSSIK: Your brother is going to die.

SHEENA: No he isn't.

HSSIK: He is. He was hit with a…particular weapon the Legion uses when it's pacifying new species. It has a one hundred percent mortality rate.

SHEENA: Bullshit.

HSSIK: The only way your brother survives is if he goes to the Legion. Now. Today. He only has a couple of days left, at most.

SHEENA: Shut up!

(SHEENA *reaches for her gun.* MICAH *grabs her arm.*)

MICAH: Sheena, no!

SHEENA: You believe this?

MICAH: Yeah. I do.

(SHEENA *stares at* MICAH. *She deflates. A long pause*)

SHEENA: Then…

MICAH: It's Legion or die.

SHEENA: Shit. Shit, shit.

MICAH: Yeah.

SHEENA: What do you want to do?

MICAH: I don't know. God, Sheena, I don't know. I don't wanna die.

SHEENA: God.

MICAH: I survived all that shit out there and now I'm gonna die here in this cave? How is that fair?

SHEENA: It's bullshit.

MICAH: It's fucking bullshit.

SHEENA: Micah, if you want to go to the Legion, I'll take you.

MICAH: Yeah?

SHEENA: Of course.

MICAH: But you'd die.

SHEENA: We don't know that for sure.

MICAH: Sheena.

SHEENA: I'm trickier than I look. If I've gotta bow and scrape and play nice for a while, I'll do it.

MICAH: You've never played nice a day in your life.

SHEENA: Sure I have.

MICAH: You beat up Jack Fisher for deadnaming me. Twice.

SHEENA: So? He was an asshole.

MICAH: You were in eighth grade! He was twice your size and the varsity quarterback.

SHEENA: He was very slow.

MICAH: I asked you to leave him alone.

SHEENA: I couldn't.

MICAH: I know. That's my point. You never know when to let something go. It's annoying as hell.

SHEENA: Gee, thanks.

MICAH: It might also be kinda badass.

(SHEENA *makes a face at* MICAH.)

MICAH: You'd see some Legion asshole picking on a human, and you wouldn't be able to help yourself. You wouldn't be able to let it go.

SHEENA: You say that like it's a bad thing.

MICAH: Not at all. But it would get you killed.

SHEENA: I'll make it work. Just until you're cured, and then we'll run.

HSSIK: No one escapes from the settlements.

SHEENA: You shut the hell up.

MICAH: No.

SHEENA: What?

MICAH: No. I'm not going.

SHEENA: Are you sure?

MICAH: Yeah. I'm sure.

(*Pause*)

SHEENA: Goddamnit.

MICAH: I know.

SHEENA: Goddamnit.

MICAH: I know.

(Long pause)

SHEENA: Okay. If that's what you want…

MICAH: It is.

HSSIK: You're throwing your life away.

MICAH: Maybe. But it's my choice.

(SHEENA stands, and turns towards HSSIK.)

SHEENA: Which means we don't need you anymore. *(She pulls out her gun.)*

HSSIK: Wait. You said you'd let me go.

SHEENA: I said if he dies, you die. And he's dying.

MICAH: Sheena—

HSSIK: I gave you the option. I did everything I could!

SHEENA: It wasn't good enough.

HSSIK: This isn't fair.

SHEENA: Didn't think you lizards went in for 'fair'.

HSSIK: That's not the point.

SHEENA: I know.

(SHEENA raises the gun, taking aim at HSSIK. A long, tense pause.)

SHEENA: Damnit. God fucking— *(She holds the gun in place a moment longer.)* You never saw us. You go back to the Legion, you tell them you got lost, and you never tell them what happened here.

(Slowly, HSSIK nods.)

SHEENA: I should—

MICAH: Let xyr go.

(SHEENA *digs the key to the padlock out and tosses it to* HSSIK.)

SHEENA: Go.

(HSSIK *hastily unlocks the chain and scrambles to the door. Xe pauses, looks back at* MICAH.)

HSSIK: I'm sorry.

MICAH: Me, too.

(HSSIK *exits, still wearing* SHEENA's *jacket.*)

SHEENA: That was the dumbest fucking thing I have ever done.

MICAH: Going soft on me, soldier girl?

SHEENA: Shut up. *(Pause)* What now?

MICAH: Wanna lay around and listen to the world fall apart?

(SHEENA *looks at* MICAH. *She nods, and goes to sit next to him as he picks up the radio. Transition: the present.*)

TSSA: It's strange.

SHEENA: What is?

TSSA: This base is so quiet now.

SHEENA: Without Badger.

TSSA: Yes.

SHEENA: Why didn't she kill you?

TSSA: Still wondering about that, are you?

SHEENA: I want to understand.

(Pause)

TSSA: I wasn't in much better shape than you were when I arrived. It's cold here in the winter, and my heating gear broke down before I could find my way. One moment, I was stumbling through the forest, trying to keep putting one foot in front of the other...

and then I was in that bed, Badger sitting on the cot
there. Closer to a human than I'd ever been in my life.
Well. A living human, anyway.
I answered every question she asked me. It felt like
I was talking for days. I thought once she was done
asking questions, that was it. She'd kill me and be done
with it. But she didn't. And a couple of days later, they
brought in a lookout who'd been wounded in a scuffle
with the Legion, and I kept them alive.

SHEENA: She let you?

TSSA: She did. And then again, and again. I couldn't
save them all, but I did what I could. I suppose it was
enough. I'm still here, after all.

SHEENA: Even though she's not.

TSSA: Even so.

(ROACH *enters, just as* AWRLL *has another coughing fit.*
ROACH *and* SHEENA *watch as* TSSA *tends her through it.*
Then, when it's over:)

TSSA: It won't be long now.

ROACH: Good.

TSSA: I should never have done this.

ROACH: It's not your fault.

TSSA: I share the blame. *(Pause)* Did you need
something?

ROACH: The last of the patrols just arrived. I figured
you two wouldn't want to miss the meeting.

SHEENA: You sure about that? Potential Legion spy,
remember?

ROACH: Oh, I'm not worried about that.

SHEENA: No? What changed?

ROACH: You've been listening to Badger long enough to know a bit about who she was. If you were Legion, we'd be screwed long since.

SHEENA: Huh.

ROACH: Picking fights with pretty much everyone who walks through the door was also a pretty good clue. Not exactly "spy trying to fit in" behavior.

SHEENA: Thought it wasn't your call.

ROACH: I'm making it my call. Tssa, you too.

TSSA: I'm not sure that's a good idea.

ROACH: You're one of us. No matter what the others think.

TSSA: I think what the others think matters a great deal.

ROACH: Give them a chance.

TSSA: I've given them many chances.

ROACH: Give them one more.

TSSA: Someone needs to keep an eye on the Soldier.

ROACH: She's tied down. And we'll lock the door behind us.
Please, Tssa. This can be the start of something, not just an ending.

(Pause)

TSSA: Fine. On your head be it.

ROACH: I can live with that.

TSSA: Let's just hope I can, too.

Scene 6

(The past. The sound of Legion ships is further away than ever. They're leaving. Radio static. The stage is empty for a moment, then SHEENA *enters with a bag of scavenged food. She puts it down and starts unpacking. She looks up, does a double-take at the spot where* MICAH *was.)*

(He's gone.)

(She stares. She drops the bag. She goes to where he was, then searches the rest of the rubble with increasing franticness, until she scrapes her hand on a rock and pulls it back, hissing in pain.)

(She's still for a moment. She looks up at the distant sound of Legion ships. She goes back to the spot on the ground. Digs something out of the pile of rubble.)

(It's her jacket, still stained with dried blood. It's cold; he's been gone a long time. SHEENA *looks at it. Beneath the jacket, she finds the radio she left with* MICAH. *The radio voices build to a cacophony, leading into the next scene.)*

RADIO 1: —can see the glow of Los Angeles burning in the western sky—

RADIO 2: —haven't seen a single survivor come out of New York. Casualty reports from Philly are piling up—

RADIO 3: —I can hear them coming. They're going to find me, any minute now. If you don't hear from me again, just know—

RADIO 4: —it's all gone, nothing left standing for miles, just fires and aliens searching what's left of downtown–

RADIO 5: —have to go now if we want to have any chance of making it. This will be the last time I'll be able to broadcast—

RADIO 6: —everything's falling apart. Not sure there's anyone out there still listening—

RADIO 7: —the Legion is overhead—it's like an eclipse, huge ships blocking out the sun for miles–

RADIO 8: —borders are completely cut off, no communication. For all we know we're the only people left on the entire planet—

RADIO 9: —don't throw your lives away. There's no use fighting anymore, they've won, it's over—

RADIO 10: —as hard as it is to acknowledge and as hard as we've fought, I think it's time we, as a nation, faced the facts: we've lost.

Scene 7

(The medbay. Late the same night. AWRLL *twists and turns, in the throes of sickness, but does not make a sound. A moment.* TSSA *enters. If she could slam the door, she clearly would.)*

(She starts for her shelves. Stops. Clenches her fists. At a loss. She lets out a long, hissing breath. She moves to tend to AWRLL. *At her touch,* AWRLL *rouses.)*

AWRLL: *(Snarled)* Shouldn't you be at your precious "meeting"?

TSSA: It was made clear to me that my presence was unwelcome.

AWRLL: Poor little Medic. Packless, as always.

TSSA: At least I can survive it.

(Pause)

AWRLL: A fair point.

TSSA: I have some human painkillers, if you want to try them.

AWRLL: Wouldn't that defeat the purpose of this whole thing? The pain is the point, is it not?

TSSA: It's gone on long enough.

AWRLL: If you truly believe that, end this.

TSSA: I can't. I'm sorry.

AWRLL: Save your apologies. I will not hear them.

(TSSA *moves away, back to her workbench, but doesn't seem to know what to do with her hands.*)

AWRLL: You may be able to survive it, but it hurts you all the same.

TSSA: What?

AWRLL: Being without a pack.

TSSA: I have a pack.

AWRLL: These humans? You call *this* a pack? Ridiculous. A broken, fractured thing. Even now, it tears apart at the seams.

TSSA: No.

AWRLL: They fight in front of me. Their enemy. The pack cannot hold.

TSSA: It will hold.

AWRLL: Impossible.

TSSA: And yet.

AWRLL: This is nothing like a true pack. Running together, moving as one. United. No true pack should have edges so sharp they cut at those within it.

TSSA: A poet as well as a Soldier.

AWRLL: You mock me.

TSSA: I meant it as a compliment.

AWRLL: Were you so lonely, in the Legion? That this is the best you could do?

TSSA: To be honest? Yes. But that's not why I'm here. I expected to be killed on sight.

AWRLL: You should have been.

TSSA: And yet here I stand.

AWRLL: Humans are irrational creatures.

TSSA: Only if you don't understand them.

AWRLL: And you do?

TSSA: Sometimes. More and more often. *(Pause)* I have a question.

AWRLL: I will tell you nothing. Just because you were once Legion—

TSSA: It's not about Badger, or anything to do with tactics or strategy. You don't have to answer it. It will change nothing.

AWRLL: Ask. I make no promises.

TSSA: What does it feel like? To be away from your pack.

AWRLL: You mock me. Again.

TSSA: No. I want to understand. Before coming here, I had no one. I've never lost anyone before.

AWRLL: Until your precious Badger.

TSSA: Yes.

(Pause)

AWRLL: I feel their absence like a hollow in my chest. Like a polar wind, blowing deep into my core. An emptiness, where I did not know I was full. I didn't know anything could hurt so much.

(A quiet moment. TSSA nods, slowly. She reaches up into her cabinets and prepares an injection, then moves to AWRLL.)

AWRLL: What is that?

TSSA: An ending.

AWRLL: I...I don't...

TSSA: It won't hurt. At least, not any more than it already does. But it's your choice. *(Pause)* What is it?

AWRLL: I don't want to die like this.

TSSA: Even if you could return to your pack, the withdrawal is too far along.

AWRLL: Not that. I accept that. But to die strapped down like an animal, in this stagnant room? If you truly want to show mercy, let me see the sky one last time.

TSSA: This is a trick.

AWRLL: No. I swear it on the bond I share with my packmates.

(A long pause)

TSSA: You'll have to cooperate. If anyone hears us...

AWRLL: I understand.

(Another moment of hesitation. Then, TSSA pockets the injector and begins removing AWRLL's restraints. As AWRLL sits up, shaky and weak, the door opens and SHEENA enters.)

(Freeze. A moment of absolute silence and stillness. Then SHEENA has her gun drawn.)

SHEENA: I knew it. I *fucking* knew it.

TSSA: Sheena, listen to me—

SHEENA: How long have you been planning this?

TSSA: It's not what it looks like.

SHEENA: Guess a traitor goes both ways, huh?

TSSA: I'm not, I—

SHEENA: You know what the worst part is? I was just starting to believe it.

TSSA: Would you please just listen?

SHEENA: Why should I? So you can make some shit up to convince me that you're not about to bring the Legion down on this entire base?

TSSA: So I can explain.

SHEENA: Same thing.

TSSA: I saved your life. Don't you owe me a chance to explain?

SHEENA: I don't owe you shit. All of this is your fault in the first place.

TSSA: My fault?

SHEENA: You. The Legion. None of this would be happening if you assholes hadn't decided you were better than us.

TSSA: I am not the Legion. I *left* the Legion.

SHEENA: Why is that, again? Because you just couldn't deal with the damage you were doing? And yet you only defected, what—two years ago? How many people did you kill before then?

TSSA: Do you think I don't remember them?

(Pause)

SHEENA: What?

TSSA: I remember every single person I have ever killed, every person I have failed to save, and there have been far too many.

SHEENA: You're saying you feel guilty.

TSSA: Of course I do.

SHEENA: Then why didn't you stop it? Why didn't you *do* something, instead of just running away?

Tssa: The same reason you're here. Because I'm one person. All I could do on my own is get killed, and then where would I be? I came because I wanted a chance—even a slim one—of actually accomplishing something with my death.

(SHEENA *hesitates. She shakes her head.*)

SHEENA: That doesn't explain what you're doing now.

Tssa: I'm doing what I think is right.

SHEENA: Fine. I'll bite. What is that, exactly?

Tssa: Mercy.

SHEENA: You're going to kill her.

Tssa: Yes.

SHEENA: Why not just do it here?

AWRLL: I asked to see the sky. (*Pause*) I will die alone. But I asked to die looking at the same sky as my pack.

SHEENA: You could've stopped this anytime. All you had to do was talk.

AWRLL: Would you?
Wouldn't you choose suffering, if it kept your pack safe? If you were captured, would you have talked?

(*Pause*)

AWRLL: You understand.

SHEENA: I'm nothing like you.

AWRLL: Denying the truth doesn't change it.

SHEENA: Fuck you. You wanna die so bad? Take one more step.

AWRLL: What happened to 'a soldier, not a murderer?'

SHEENA: Guess they're the same thing after all.

Tssa: Sheena.

SHEENA: This dog doesn't deserve mercy.

TSSA: Who are you to decide that?

SHEENA: I'm the only human here.
I can't believe… They let you live, and this is how you pay them back?

(TSSA *laughs, short and sharp and humorless.*)

SHEENA: Something funny?

TSSA: Two years. Two years I've been with this Rebellion. How long do I have to pay them back for? How much, exactly, do I owe them?

SHEENA: More for every moment you keep breathing.

TSSA: When does it end? I've done terrible things, yes. But so has this Rebellion. So have you, I'm sure.

SHEENA: Not like you. You fuckers just take, and take, and take. My friends. My parents. My brother. Everyone I have ever given a damn about, you've taken away from me.

TSSA: It has to stop, Sheena. Someone has to draw the line.

SHEENA: And you think it's going to be you.

TSSA: No one else seems to be stepping up.

SHEENA: If your motives are so pure, why don't Ibis and Roach know about this? Why go behind their backs?

TSSA: You know as well as I do that they'd never allow this. They're grieving, and angry, and they've spent too long fighting.
So have you.

SHEENA: You know nothing about me.

TSSA: I know what grief looks like. Exhaustion. Fury. I've seen it on every person in this crew. I see it in you.

SHEENA: Shut *up*.

(TSSA *turns to* AWRLL *and starts to help her up.*)

SHEENA: Stop.

TSSA: No.

SHEENA: I said *stop.*

TSSA: If you think it's the right thing to do, shoot me.

(SHEENA *tracks* TSSA *and* AWRLL *with the gun until they are out of the room. A long moment of silence.*)

SHEENA: Damnit.

Scene 8

(*The present.* SHEENA *perches on the bed, cleaning her pistol.* IBIS *and* ROACH *aren't happy.*)

ROACH: She just left?

SHEENA: Yep.

IBIS: You just…let her go?

SHEENA: Yep.

IBIS: You didn't stop her?

SHEENA: Nope.

IBIS: Why the hell not?

(*No answer*)

ROACH: Sheena? Why didn't you?

SHEENA: I couldn't.

IBIS: What's that supposed to mean?

SHEENA: I couldn't pull the trigger. Call me weak, fuck it, but I couldn't do it. What is that saying? Stupidity is doing the same thing over and over again and expecting a different outcome.

ROACH: I think the saying is insanity, actually.

SHEENA: Whatever. You'd think I'd have learned by now.

ROACH: What are you talking about?

SHEENA: It's a really, really long story.

(Pause)

IBIS: We need to move the base.

ROACH: To where? Where the hell would we go? The Legion's still close; they'd see if we all suddenly started running in the other direction.

IBIS: You have a better plan? Camp out here and wait for the bomb to drop?

ROACH: I don't like it either, but...I don't think she'd betray us.

IBIS: Then you're a fool.

ROACH: Maybe. But I'm the fool who's running this joint, now, so.
If you want to go, I won't blame you. Give people the option to go with you. Maybe a smaller group could slip out.

TSSA: That won't be necessary.

(All three look up. TSSA *stands in the doorway. Pause.)*

TSSA: *(To* ROACH*)* Congratulations.

ROACH: Uh, thanks.

TSSA: I'm surprised, considering how things were going when I...left.

ROACH: We need to be better than that. I just...helped everyone else see that, I guess.

IBIS: Tssa. What did you do?

TSSA: Mercy.

IBIS: You put all of us in danger.

TSSA: It was a calculated risk.

IBIS: It wasn't your risk to take.

TSSA: Be that as it may, I took it.

(*Pause*)

ROACH: Okay.

IBIS: Okay?

ROACH: Okay.

TSSA: Thank you.

ROACH: I just hope you know what you're doing.

TSSA: I do.

ROACH: In the meantime, I'm late for a strategy meeting.
Ibis. You coming?

IBIS: You want me there?

ROACH: Yeah. You too, Tssa. Sheena.

SHEENA: Inviting the whole base, huh?

ROACH: More or less.

TSSA: That's…a change.

ROACH: A good one, I think.
I'm not Badger. I never will be. I'm not even sure I want to be the one making the hard decisions, let alone all the other ones, but I'll do it when I have to. When we have the time, though…we're all good at different things. When we can, we should all be making decisions. Together.

SHEENA: Very kumbaya.

ROACH: There are worse things to be.
Anyway, like I said. I'm late.

(*They start to exit.*)

ROACH: Oh, and Sheena?

SHEENA: Yeah?

ROACH: Better come up with that moniker. You're going to need it. *(Exits)*

IBIS: Did she say anything?

TSSA: Hmm?

IBIS: The Soldier. Did she say anything, at the end? About Badger?

TSSA: No. By the time we got outside…she was too far gone.
For what it's worth, I was going to ask her.

IBIS: Thank you.

TSSA: And I'm sorry. I didn't always agree with Badger, but I respected her.

IBIS: Her name was Rachel.
I don't want to be the only one left who remembers her.

SHEENA: Everyone with a radio remembers her.

IBIS: They remember Badger, Rebellion leader. But she was so much more.

SHEENA: Tell me about her. When you're ready.

IBIS: Maybe I will.

(A moment. IBIS exits.)

TSSA: How's your arm?

SHEENA: You're really gonna ask me that now?

TSSA: I am a Medic.

SHEENA: It's fine.

TSSA: Good. *(She moves to her workbench.)*

SHEENA: You're not going to the meeting?

TSSA: I think I'll pass on this one. It feels a bit like pushing my luck. What about you?

SHEENA: I'm not much of a planner. More of a munitions kind of gal.

TSSA: I've certainly gotten that impression. *(From the workbench, she produces a vial of blood.)*

SHEENA: That's Roach's?

TSSA: Yes.

SHEENA: You never told me what you were doing with it.

(Pause)

TSSA: Did you see any of the big cities, after... After?

SHEENA: After you destroyed them? No. Not personally. But I heard...

TSSA: What?

SHEENA: That no one made it out.

TSSA: No one.

SHEENA: That the New York subway is full of bodies.

TSSA: Yes. Do you know what killed them?

SHEENA: Some kind of Legion weapon. One hundred percent mortality rate.

TSSA: Yes, well...turns out it's not quite one hundred.

SHEENA: What?

TSSA: Has Roach told you where they come from?

SHEENA: I bet you're about to tell me.

TSSA: New York City.

(Pause)

SHEENA: 'They haven't managed to kill me yet.'

TSSA: The only case I've ever heard of.

SHEENA: So the blood...

TSSA: If I can pinpoint what allowed Roach to survive, maybe I can stop this.

SHEENA: You want to stop it?

TSSA: We may have made it, but we never meant for it to be used this way.

SHEENA: Yeah, well. The road to hell, good intentions, all of that.

TSSA: The weapon isn't common knowledge outside of the Rebellion. How do you know of it?

SHEENA: The Legion hit my hometown with it. I was still at the base. Things were falling apart anyway, so when I heard they'd hit my home, I just—ran. My parents didn't... They died before I even got there. My brother...

TSSA: I'm sorry, Sheena.

SHEENA: Guess it's a good thing I didn't pull the trigger this time, either.

TSSA: What?

SHEENA: Skip it. Maybe I'll tell you one day.

(Pause)

TSSA: Thank you. For not pulling the trigger.

SHEENA: Yeah, yeah.
By the way, I decided on a callsign.

TSSA: What?

SHEENA: For the radio.

TSSA: Oh.

SHEENA: Yeah. Shrike.

TSSA: That's a...bird?

SHEENA: A little tiny one. Looks adorable, but it's also known as the "butcher bird".

Tssa: Fitting.

Sheena: I thought so.

Tssa: I thought you said you didn't have anyone left to protect.

Sheena: Yeah, well. You never know.

(Blackout. Radio static)

END OF PLAY

RADIO VOICES

At least 8 voices, pre-recorded.

Hearing a number of different voices over the radio is key to making the world of the Legion Cycle feel well-populated outside the confines of this specific story. The original production of Shrike had a group of 8 actors record the radio voices ahead of time and those recordings became part of the sound design. That breakdown is below and is a suggestion for how other productions could tackle this element. No production should have fewer than 8 actors recording the radio lines. If you'd like to have more than 8 voice actors, feel free to further divide voice lines, except from characters who are specifically named *(such as Croc, Hawk, the scout Ibis talks to, etc)* who should be consistent throughout.

General note: All Scene 6 voices are different characters than any other appearance of the same voice actor. All reappearances within Scene 6 are also different people.

Actor 1:
Scene 1—RADIO 1—Rebellion member, not part of Badger's crew
Scene 3—RADIO 2—Newscaster
Scene 6—RADIO 10

Actor 2:
Scene 1—RADIO 2—Rebellion member
Scene 4—RADIO 2—Rebellion member, could be the

same or different as Scene 1.

Scene 6—RADIO 2 and RADIO 8

Actor 3:
Scene 1—RADIO 3—Rebellion member
Scene 2—RADIO 2—Rebellion member, different from previous
Scene 6—RADIO 1 and RADIO 7

Actor 4:
Scene 1—RADIO 4—Hawk. Western Rebel leader. Older woman.
Scene 2—RADIO 1—Hawk again.
Scene 6—RADIO 9

Actor 5:
Scene 1—RADIO 5—Rebel scout in Badger's crew.
Scene 4—RADIO 5—same Rebel scout.
Scene 6—RADIO 5

Actor 6:
Scene 1—RADIO 6—Academic/historian vibes. Could be a Rebel, could be someone else.
Scene 4—RADIO 1—Academic/historian vibes. Could be a different person, or the same.
Scene 6—RADIO 3

Actor 7:
Scene 2—RADIO 4—Croc, southern Rebel leader. Woman, Southern accent.
Scene 5—RADIO 1—Croc again.
Scene 6—RADIO 4

Actor 8:
Scene 2—RADIO 3—Rebellion member
Scene 3—RADIO 1—Badger
Scene 6—RADIO 6

IBIS: (should be recorded by the same person who plays Ibis onstage)
Scene 1—RADIO 7
Scene 4—RADIO 4

GLOSSARY OF LEGION CYCLE TERMS

Aurora—the noncombatant arm of the Rebellion. Responsible for supply runs, scientific work on captured Legion tech, etc.

Badger—Rebellion leader in the eastern US. If the Rebellion has a figurehead, it's her. Missing in action.

Brute—Large, tank-like aliens with thick armor plating. Usually seen in ground combat.

Command—the alien species that leads the Legion. Not much is known about them.

Croc—Rebellion leader in the southern US.

Ember—the combat arm of the Rebellion. Led by Badger, Hawk, and Croc.

Hawk—Rebellion leader in the western US. Cautious.

Legionnaire's Code—Loyalty, Obedience, Strength. The unifying rule by which the Legion operates.

Medic—Reptilian aliens that generally work alone. Responsible for caring for the injured and some related scientific work within the Legion.

(the) Rebellion—the human resistance to the Legion's occupation. Consists of three main branches, operating out of many decentralized cells. Rebellion members use animal monikers to hide their identities.

Scout—Avian aliens that work in flocks. Responsible for scouting new terrain and patrolling controlled terrain. Humans often refer to them derogatorily as "birdbrains".

Soldier—Canine aliens that work in packs. Responsible for ground combat.

Tracker—Ratlike aliens that generally work alone. Responsible for tracking down runaways.

(the) Web—the observation arm of the Rebellion. Web members watch and report, but generally do not actively participate in Rebellion actions.